The Stonegate Devil

Acknowledgements

Many thanks to the editors of the following, where some of these poems first appeared: *52 Anthology, Acumen, Agenda, The Black Light Engine Room, Magma, Nutshells and Nuggets, The Interpreter's House, Ink Sweat and Tears, Schooldays* anthology (Paper Swans, 2015), *The North, Poetry Review, Poetry Scotland, The Garden (Otley Wordfest), And Other Poems, Gumbo, The Lightship Anthology 2012, Poetry Advent Calendar 2012, Keats Shelley Review, The Hippocrates Prize Anthology 2014.*

'Eleanor Marx translates Madame Bovary' won first prize in the 2014 Torbay Poetry Competition, 'On the Carpet' won second prize in the 2014 Wells Festival of Literature Competition, 'Wish I'd never met you' won third prize in the 2013 Ilkley Literature Festival Competition, 'In My Wallet' won second prize in the 2012 Elmet Poetry Competition and 'Tom Makes His Mark' won third prize in the 2011 Keats Shelley Award.

I would also like to thank Jo Bell and my friends at the 52 group, the York Stanza, Leeds University Poetry Group, Stuart Pickford, Lydia Harris, Liz Cashdan, Jennifer Copley, Clare Crossman and Jo Stoney, John Glenday, Colette Bryce, Antony Dunn and Ian Duhig for invaluable advice.

The Stonegate Devil
Carole Bromley

smith|doorstop

Published 2015 by
smith|doorstop Books
The Poetry Business
Bank Street Arts
32-40 Bank Street
Sheffield S1 2DS
www.poetrybusiness.co.uk

Copyright © Carole Bromley 2015

ISBN 978-1-910367-54-4

Carole Bromley hereby asserts her moral right to be identified as
the author of this book.

British Library Cataloguing-in-Publication Data.
A catalogue record for this book is available from the
British Library.

Typeset by Utter
Printed by Printondemand.com
Cover image: The Stonegate Devil
Author photo: Michael J Oakes photography

smith|doorstop is a member of Inpress,
www.inpressbooks.co.uk. Distributed by Central Books Ltd.,
99 Wallis Road, London E9 5LN.

The Poetry Business is an Arts Council
National Portfolio Organisation

Supported by
ARTS COUNCIL
ENGLAND

Contents

For my mother and for Ros

The Stonegate Devil

He's seen it all: mummers, buskers,
guildsmen pulling carts with wobbling tableaux
of flood, famine, crucifixion;

a couple choosing a ring in Walker and Preston's,
a man hurrying another man's wife
down the alley to Ye Olde Starre Inne,

drunks vomiting in the snickelway,
the purple cyclist on his purple bike,
going nowhere.

The devil's crouched on that ledge
since Coffee Yard was Langton Lane
and Stonegate the Street of the Printers.

He doesn't need the gear in *Old Guys Rule,*
wears a black chain and a pair of horns,
his skin boiled lobster,

those hands on his knees a man's hands,
his feet the feet of a goat
and, though you can see his ribs,

he has no appetite for the eggs
in *Bettys* display, the chocolate otter,
the hare or the candy daffodils,

does not thirst for the spirits
in the window of Evil Eye
or the barrels in Trembling Madness

where the missing student on the poster
Megan, we would love to hear from you
smiles her pretty smile.

formerly *Mad Alice Lane*

The hanged woman haunts
Lund's Court which today
is all grafitti and pigeon shit.
You can see how it was,
the house with the gas lamp,
a sunfilled courtyard,
lace curtains at an upper window.
A handy short cut to Swinegate
and the old Mission Hall,
Oscar's, el piano, nail bar one
but you wouldn't nip through here
after dark alone.
Executed for poisoning
her husband or possibly
just for having the gall
to go round the bend,
she wanders the ginnel,
muttering recipes:
dead toad and camomile,
the juice of cuckoo pint
chased down with honey.
A raw bad egg, a brace
of pheasant, the shot
still in, a steamed sponge
pudding laced with lead,
a glass of grog
with something green,
the daintiest petits fours
you've ever seen,
their soft centres filled
with pure strychnine
washed down with ale
tinged with dropwort,

briony and aconite.
Alice doesn't eat a bite,
just watches him tuck in
then runs like hell up Petergate.

Beningbrough Hall

I'd like to know what 'snippets of tittle tattle'
the laundress tucked in among the goffered shirts,
broderie anglaise petticoats and lace bibs
sent in a box from London.

I wonder if she ever took a swig of the gin
that was meant for removing grease stains
or fought off the advances of the messenger boy
with a swipe of that mangle bat.

I bet they never let her sit in the East Formal garden
with its whites, pinks and blues, its views
of the south lawn, parkland straight out of Watteau,
that haha keeping the black cows out.

Purple is king in the old rose garden
with its salvia, ceonothus, campanula,
the only sounds wind like water in the trees,
footsteps on gravel, an old man's cough.

In the walled garden, where catmint and lady's mantle
tumble under arches of espaliered pear, girls in long frocks
and boys in peaked caps play hoop and ball,
the laundry clock strikes one, even the rhubarb knows its place.

On The Carpet

The carpet is threadbare and brown
and my feet, in their red Startrite sandals,
suddenly small. There is an earwig
marching across the pattern. It must seem
like a hundred miles to him. I don't like earwigs
but I leave him be.

There is nobody else in the room,
just the headmaster, the earwig and me.
If I look very hard at the earwig
or at the cut out flowers on my toes
which have a little smear of Cherry Blossom
still in the middle leaf, I'll be alright.

But the earwig has reached the edge
of the carpet and it's not alright.
Mr Mapplebeck's voice is very loud.
I can smell his coffee breath.
'I'm going to ask you one more time.
Was it you that stole from Woolworth's?'

And I can see the counter at the big shop
the spinning top, the clockwork mouse,
the striped plastic windmill and, in my head,
my hand is reaching. I'm crying now,
I didn't do it. I didn't do it, though now
I'm not so sure any more. Perhaps I did.

Perhaps it was me. Perhaps I'm a thief
but I won't say yes and I won't look up
at Mr Mapplebeck who is a giant.
I'll be the earwig who keeps on marching
though it will take him all afternoon
to reach the window and he hasn't any shoes.

The Doll With a Hole in its Hand

I'm seven today and no-one's bothered.
They're too busy putting things in tea chests.
Even David Horsley's more interested in the van;
I rode on his trike and he never noticed.
Bridget and Patricia wouldn't play hopscotch
because they wanted to sit on the wall and watch.

Who'll turn the rope with me tomorrow?
England, Ireland, Scotland, Wales
Russia, Prussia, Germany.
I wrote my name on the bedroom wall.
Mum looks as if she'll burst; Auntie Josie says
That baby'd better not come early.

Mum's worn the same dress for weeks now
and the hem goes right up at the front.
I can't remember when she was thin.
Grandma came round with a present
in a big white box with a ribbon;
she couldn't stay long because of the shop.

Really I'm too big for dolls but the removal man
said it was a bobby dazzler. She's a fairy
with a gold dress and a hole in her hand.
I tried to tell them she'd lost her wand
but grandma said, *Maybe she's an angel, pet,*
and angels don't have wands so I said

What about the hole? and I'm still looking.
I don't want to go to the new house. Di skips about
singing 17 Well Lane Willerby like it's real
but I'm scared of wells. If your ball goes down,
you can't get it back unless you kiss
a frog and let him sleep in your bed all night.

Gran's Staircase

I was Violet Elizabeth Bott, screaming
and the burnt pan stood, unwashed,
on the draining board.

She'd go to and fro through
the shop door or into the kitchen
and, halfway up the stairs,

I'd be watching. In that house
I was always sick. Swallowing can be
so hard. You have no idea.

Hawkeye

She hated me. It was a second hand hate
meant for my sister who smirked.
I didn't smirk but I did daydream
and I didn't like speaking up
so one day she marched the class
from Norwood House to the school hall
with its honours boards and its silence
and made me read the poem again
only louder, louder, LOUDER.

Exasperated by my timidity
she ordered the class into the corridor
and said I was to read it till they could hear
through the wall. So I shook on that stage
and I did speak up though only
the long dead girls in gold could hear me.

First Kiss

The first time anyone kissed me
was Valentine's Day, 1962.
He knew what he was doing
and I didn't, even though I'd practised
on the bathroom mirror
and on my pillow case
and on the back of my arm.

Anyway that first time
I was ready and willing
to try the real thing.
There were no cards in my desk,
they were for the girls
with the back-combed hair,
Janet Tansley and June Smith.

So when Mick and Jim
sent a message to the girls
in the needlework room
at lunch-time, I got up
and went. I fancied Jim
but it was Mick I kissed,
with his quiff and cut off tie

and he knew how to kiss
but the best of it was
the trembling. Afterwards
it was like a pact, something
new had been spoken.
I moved on to Jim,
a woman and he knew it.

Touch

There wasn't a lot of it in our house.
We learned to live without

though I do remember one time
when my friend, Rosemary, died

and, on the same day, my boyfriend
told someone to tell me we were through

which was a shame since he
was one of the first people

in my whole life to touch me
and I loved it. That night my father

asked me to come down from my room
and watch the news with them.

Three and a half inches of snow
had fallen that day in Alamo.

I lay on the sofa while dad stroked my hair
like an awkward teenager

and, a quarter of a million miles away,
the Russians made the first soft landing on the moon.

Fond

When I said I was fond of you
I didn't mean like of ballet,

I meant fond as in tender,
as in fond embrace.

My dad used the word differently;
Don't be fond he'd say,

exasperated by some evidence
of foolishness

as if he couldn't believe
I was serious.

Good job I never told him
my fondest hopes,

I'd have covered my ears;
I was daft about you.

Ghazal

I love talking to stones, love it, love it,
they may not listen but I rise above it.

Talking to a river's too easy somehow,
less of a competition. Stones give it

their all; rivers, on the whole, just chatter.
(but don't tell them that, they won't have it).

If there's a point you want to get across
to a stone, don't bother, save it

for when you're talking to a river.
Never interrupt a stone; they'll not forgive it,

they'll say you talk too much then take
your share of the time and halve it.

Rivers won't fight, but show them an obstacle,
they'll move it.

while a stone thinks its viewpoint's all that counts
and will stand and prove it.

But, Carole, talk to the stones all you like;
the river will hear you. Believe it.

Eleanor Marx Translates Madame Bovary

London,1884. She's looking up Prussic acid,
her mind half on that evening and her lover,
the one her father doesn't trust.

Emma sends the maid out yet again
to Rodolphe's house to enquire
if there's any reply to her message.

Eleanor's not sure whether *club foot* is right
and fears she's made the husband
less than sympathetic.

Later, there's a meeting of the Socialist League
and she's looking forward to the paper
from that nice Dr. Aveling.

The Lepidopterist Falls In Love

He can't resist her flimsy frocks,
that slim, firm body.
Crazy for her black eyes,

he stalks her,
hangs around her favourite haunts
with net and killing bottle.

No-one else's specimen comes close;
only the best parchment will do,
the sharpest pin.

John Keats' Ring

Fanny wore it on a string
those last months, oh she wore it
against her untouched skin -
she had his heart. He swore it.

Her mother would have disapproved;
he'd bare enough to live;
she took this token of his love,
all he had to give

and kept it hidden in her gown,
warm against her breast,
the solitaire of almandine,
until he was at rest.

They cut her hair when she fell sick,
she'd neither sleep nor eat,
but dressed herself in widow's black
and all night walked the Heath.

Tom Makes His Mark

Thomas Clarke, Plumber and Glazier
July 4th - 1794, aged 15

I did it for a dare and to win a girl. She said
I never would but I proved her wrong,
chose the horse's arse, bottom left
on the last panel, the one about the apocalypse.

I've a handsome hand but big and this
was the widest expanse of clear glass to write on.
I was proud of my curled initial, though my hand
shook a little when I heard the master coming
and the writing slopes downhill
to the right like on the board at school.

Anyway, after all those back-breaking months
of grozing, of staining my fingers
with lunar caustic and Cousin's rose,
of straining my eyes repainting chain mail,
an ape's tooth, the turned-down mouth
of a knight, the way I saw it, I'd a right.

And who was to know? Once the panel
was hoisted into place and the scaffolding
removed no-one would see the details
till dirt and damp and loosening glue
had undone our handiwork and that
wouldn't be for a century or two.

I like to think of an apprentice
all those years hence, reading my words.
I wish I could tell him about the night,
oh the night, I spent with the girl.

Oranges

There were never oranges
like the one you peeled for me
that first night, paring the rind,
removing with a surgeon's skill
every trace of white.

Zest filled the air.
You watched me sink my teeth in,
laughed as I posted a segment
into your mouth. Afterwards
you lit one of your father's cigarettes.

I closed my eyes and breathed in
smoke, the scent of oranges, you.

In My Wallet

My favourite photo of you was taken
by your ex-girlfriend. I like the look on your face
which seems to say everything you swear
you've only said to me but I don't believe you.
There's something about the way you're standing
on the Heath with your collar turned up
and your sleeves rolled back as the sun sets.
Shortly after, you dumped her for me
just as I (though I never told you this)
dumped someone I'd thought I loved for you.
Your expression's the same as the one
on your face the night I came home drunk
from dancing and flirting with someone else
and you fucked me right there on the carpet.

Flighty

When, all those years ago, your brother
took you aside and warned you

I wondered how he knew something that I
had not yet learned myself

and, later, when I proved him right
and you forgave me, I thought

perhaps, after all, it was love
he was afraid of, or flight.

Field Day

i.m. Richard Aveling Bromley

When your brother drowned
swinging across the Rawthey
while the others stood in line
and the master in charge
realised too late
how swollen the river was,
how short the rope,

he took down with him
into the fast-flowing water
his love of churches and cycling,
his place at Cambridge,
his parents' hopes,
one brother's dreams,
another's peace of mind.

Lost in the swirling, icy flood
the girls he'd never kiss,
the sons he wouldn't have,
the prizes he wouldn't win,
the photographs he'd not take,
the friends and the pubs
and the flowers and the birds

and when he came to rest
near Briggflatts, his body
caught in those reeds,
his hair floating, his strong legs
moving with the current,
he couldn't know, in that silence,
how the world was changed.

Rendezvous

after Dennis O'Driscoll

I am in Stonegate
expecting to meet you at 4

You are in The Shambles
expecting to meet me at 4

I have shopping bags that lengthen my arms
you have Jonathan on your shoulders

It's Christmas and *I'm Dreaming*
blasts out from Ye Olde Starre Inn

In Giovanni's doorway a busker sings *Jingle Bells*
flat cap at his feet

It is five past four
and no sign of you

It is five past four
and no sign of me

You may have forgotten your watch
I may have bumped into someone

You may be in A&E
I may be under a bus

A White Christmas
is on a loop

The busker has been moved on
flat cap on his head

You have got the front door key
I have got the supper

We must stop not meeting like this.

Wish I'd never met you

All I have to do, they tell me, is
close my eyes and picture the last time;
in the Bonding Warehouse,
you in your black jacket with those eyes
I have to come at slant
if I'm to cope with them at all.

This isn't working yet. But wait.
Maybe if we press rewind to the bit
where you stroke my hair afterwards
or, better still, to five minutes
before that. No, no, keep going
past the bit where you read the poem,

on, on to where we run backwards
down the hill in the snow
to the taxi. Stop when we get
to the bench. That's it. Look,
I'm throwing my gloves in the Foss,
you're easing yours onto my hands.

Keep going. Watch me spit
the Southern Comfort into your glass,
do your moonwalk to the jukebox,
silence the opening bars of *SOS*,
I'll run to the exit, we'll back out
hand in hand, I'll unlock my bike,

you'll be in such a hurry
to the bus stop you won't even wave
and when I get home the key
will jump into the waiting lock,
the back door will swing open
and everyone will still be at the table.

Cloughton
after Andrew Waterhouse

We did not go there that day,
or any other. You never helped me
over the fence, I never made the joke
about why the bullocks were angry,
you never laughed *I suppose I would.*
There was no rock shaped like a sofa,
no man chipping fossils from the cliff.

It was not my birthday. You did not
hand me a silver box of chocolates,
a green bottle of Mosel so we couldn't have
passed it back and forth all afternoon.
Look it up. It wasn't windy that day,
the tide didn't come back in for hours
so how could we have skimmed stones?

Cormorants are never found on that stretch
of coast, wild garlic does not grow there.
A hare is a rare thing in those parts
so how could you have pointed him out
running, running in that field? I tell you,
you're mistaken. It wasn't me. We
never went there. That day or any other.

Passageway Books

Why does the door always creak?
Will he ever go through
those boxes of magazines?
Taxidermy for Beginners £3.50,
a ten volume encyclopaedia
with MAL to ORA missing. Offers.
Atlases of vanished worlds,
dictionaries that have never heard
of smart phones, iPads, even teletext.
Crime novels someone took on holiday
and never opened, six pristine copies
of *Birthday Letters* in hardback
and then – the pocket Milton
I bought for you. I handed it over
in the Cock and Bottle, didn't write in it
because it was so beautiful.
Still £25 as if I'd never gone there,
as if you and I had never been.

The Raggedy Bush

Dun Laoghaire. The name sparks to life
the day we disembarked, drove south

to County Wexford, hired bikes, explored
from the lanes of Kilkenny, down to the shores

of New Ross where your ancestors were from.
One set sail for India, married a local woman

and stayed. You wanted me to find
some trace of the family he left behind;

a name on a gravestone, perhaps. I looked
but it was a fool's errand you took me on.

Might as well look on the raggedy bush
for your grandfather's sock, make a wish

on a fluttering handkerchief, scarf, glove -
wherever you are, travel safe, my love.

Edge

Well, I could comb the beach for ever
and not find what I'm looking for,
just the evidence of other lives,
their fleshy, pulsing selves vanished,
the walls echoing with kittiwakes.

I could feel the shock of the waves,
the fragments of broken shell
cutting my soles, could sniff
the air and it would not be there,
this thing I'm seeking:

this edge, this treading the line
that comes and goes and comes again
and never rests: cup your hands
and holler out to sea. The ship on the horizon
will keep on sailing away.

Sochi

for Ann Atkinson

Stuck indoors. Flicking between events
on the sort of afternoon when you could ski
down our avenue, thinking of you,
how that day in the hospital when you made
so little sense but were glad to see Jo,
so glad to see Jo, you said you didn't give a flying fuck
about the Olympics. Your wake at the Maynard
after the weeping, hugging of smokers
in that cold wind, in the bar where Lucas used
the polished floor as a skating rink, we joked
about how it would make a great Olympic event.
Annie, I'd rather watch the flying fuck, or even
take part in it than be sitting here, remote in hand,
flicking between the curling and the skeleton.

Companions

All the Japanese passengers lay down
on the lower deck for a snooze on the floor
with a foam brick for a pillow;
even my daughter had adopted
this strange custom, born of overwork
and a need to fit in sleep around the edges.
Their shoes, all facing the same way,
lined up at the edge of the matting.

I was far too excited, wanted to see
Kagoshima slip away, feel the spray
on my face. I stood at the prow end
between the sea and the sky,
Yakoshima not even in sight yet
or the smaller islands on the way.
It was not silent; the huge ship's engine
and the smash of hull on water saw to that.

Then I saw them, the flying fish,
muscle into the air, perform
a wriggling parabola to defy
the Earth's pull and then plummet.
It seemed they would win
but then the shoal was in our wake
and there was nothing visible
but the rise and fall of that iron railing.

@paultheweatherman

I'm in love with Paul the weather man.
Never miss Look North, must get my fix
of orange shirts and pink ties.
I would kill to have a man with his laugh,
that cleft chin, those dimples. I love it
when he tells himself a joke
and laughs so much he can't go on.

The way he says isobars does it for me,
that sweeping gesture to indicate
the direction of the wind sends shivers
down my spine. I have to take an extra sip
of peppermint tea. Every day I tweet him:
selfies of me in sun and rain,
me in fog and snow, me in sea fret and drizzle.

A Paean to Solitude

Oh the joys of irregular hours,
of writing till three in the morning
and breakfasting at noon,
of dining on can't-be-arsed leftovers
washed down with copious amounts
of whatever you fancy and no-one
to point out the unit count. The bliss
of rediscovering all those hours
you've missed, and no-one
to ring and interrupt. Just you
and a glass or two or three or four
and a poem humming in the air
like the first fat bee on the almond.

On the Road to Sheepwash

The air is so still. Still as me sitting here
half-way up the slope. I should know what birds
those are, the *whit-whit*, the *Susie Susie*,
the one like a man whistling his dog, the *churl-churl*.
Now that's the throttled squawk of a pheasant.
Let them sing away, not minding me,
buttock on thistle, hot sun on the back of my neck.
The *purrrr-rrrip* continues, the one like a whistle
almost too high for the human ear. Those cows
are painted on that meadow; the only thing moving
is a white van on the horizon. The hands
on my watch are in no more of a hurry
than the clouds are, or that thistledown. Listen.
tsoee, tsoee. Pinking shears cutting through silk.

Stylist

My hairdresser doesn't really get poetry;
he's into Thai boxing, but he does ask about it.
We have these weird conversations
while we pretend there's a point
in even talking about a new style.
He tells me about his broken nose,
how the A&E consultant lost patience
when he went straight out and got it broken again
and I tell him about stuff that's alien
like doing readings to ten people
and spending more on a course
than I earn in a year. He's given up
trying to understand why I write
and I've given up trying to understand
the appeal of getting the shit kicked out of you.
I suggest the two activities are not so different;
he suggests a little layering at the sides.

The Walk

Slithering onto the track
clutching at branches
we laugh, you choosing
the safety of that ridge of deep snow,
me risking the hard-crack ice
of the ruts, we find a horse,
his breath hanging in the air.

By the barn which we can't get into
because of the drift against
the door, we opt to go further,
to leave the writing because
the woods are so lovely,
every twig tensed with snow.

And, just beyond the lake,
you tell me about the abortion
eight weeks ago, how your mum
cried when you told her.
We walk on up the slope,
ice breaking like glass
under our stout warm boots.

Morning Prayer

A prod in a Catholic school,
I was easily spotted -
my voice went on
when everyone else's stopped.

I couldn't get the hang
of crossing myself either;
my form got used to me
giving the Our Father a miss.

Just once I went through with it
when their friend killed his brother
with a bread knife at breakfast;
they stayed with me to the amen.

Margaret Clitheroe's Hand

The hand's too much for me.
To my pupils, used to such relics,
it's a joke. When the Pope came
and canonised her, they say
he received one of her fingers
as a memento. The lads in the back row
reckon he's collecting bodyparts
and all he needs is a torso.

The story, of course, is what counts.
That martyrdom under a weighted door
for the crime of harbouring priests.
I never walk down the Shambles
without thinking of her, how she sent
her shoes to her daughters
so they could follow in her footsteps
and went to her death barefoot.

Oberon's Cloak

I'm not saying that you weren't good
though it would serve you right
for the way you cut me dead in Waitrose,

you in your Armani suit. You saw me alright.
I haven't changed that much in twenty years
though you have, Eddie. You have.

We used to say, Mrs G and I, that one day
you'd come back a Sir and tell the other kids
how the golden cloak was just the beginning.

I still have the homework you wrote
about how you couldn't bear to take it off
and be just plain Edward again.

Plumbers

They're like gold dust. They arrive whistling,
shake their heads, say 'Who fitted that?'
and 'I don't know, love' and 'It'll cost you'.

They take long breaks, bring their own snap
which they eat with unwashed hands
as if they'd never heard of germs.

They are unfazed by your shit;
it's all in a day's work. Nice ones let you
fill a kettle first. These days they could be

your old Year Tens. They catch themselves
saying 'Miss'. You can't remember their names.
After they've gone the water comes in burps.

School Gates

is Matilda and Martha's favourite game.
They can play it for hours. It goes like this.
I have to be the teacher by the French window,
while they take it in turns to be the mother
dropping her daughter off and picking her up.
Nothing happens in between.
Just the meeting and the parting. Dropping off
is the hard bit, whoever's being mother
brings her daughter in, hangs up her school bag,
leaves her with her snack, takes teacher aside
and tells her it's a headache today
or she's been up in the night with earache
and might have to be picked up early.
The snack is a plastic carrot or a pepper
then it's time for the bell and the mother
runs in, arms open wide, hugs her child
and they stand for a while like that.
Then it's morning and the whole thing
starts again. Being a teacher's a piece of cake.

Poem with a Satsuma in it

There is no sunset can rival
the particular shade of its skin

no sunrise the pimpled texture
no noon-glow the zing.

There can never be too many
satsumas in poems,

each segment a stanza,
every metaphor a pip.

I open a book of them
and my mouth waters

even before I've tasted
the opening line.

My grand-daughter
can't say the word,

just points
more, more, more

Meeting
for Elijah Joseph

In the corridor a woman,
open-mouthed at her own death.

In the ward you, wide-eyed
with a different kind of surprise.

I carry you to the window
and show you the world

or the world as it is today,
The Stray in mist, a line of cars,

mauve spears of crocus,
the first bud on a chestnut

and you listen with the patience
of a man hearing a story

for the umpteenth time
and study your grandmother's face.

Where did you come from
little scrap with a big name?

Mabel

The two syllables rise
new as soap bubbles
trembling from a wand

your first cry
enters the startled world,
your name is inked on a bracelet

and suddenly here it is
your face materialising
on my phone.

Granny's Ghazal

*For Billy, Lotte, Josephine, Teddy, Jemima, Matilda,
Eleanor, James, Elijah, Martha, Tabitha and Mabel*

Though you nudge me towards the grave
I forgive you.

I'm one, two, three, four, five ... twelve times blest
to have you –

I didn't do the maths. Never dreamt there'd be
so many of you.

I'm sorry I can't arrange that nothing
will ever grieve you

or that when you're being truthful
people will believe you

or that when your boat is sinking I'll be there
to save you

but I'd like to make just one good poem
to leave you

when I'm gone into the earth or, who knows,
the sky above you

so close your eyes and imagine. This is the gift
I would give you.

Twiggy

I knew you had really gone
when you bought the whippet.
It wasn't the four grandchildren
or the work-bench you sent off for
from a craftsman in Perth
that stands, polished, virginal
in the corner of your vast garage
and which one day will be worn and scratched
and well-loved like your dad's.
No, it was the spiky thing that leapt
for your love, that yelped in the laundry
for the vanished mother, then next day
started practising circuits of the yard.

Baz Luhrman's Rug

He'd set his heart on it for Gatsby's sitting room
but you came along next day and bought it;
it was perfect for the gap next to your table.

You agreed to rent it to him
for two hundred dollars a day
though it meant the floor was bare for months.

Stained now, a little worn, not quite so blue
but you can always fast forward to Daisy,
curling her little feet on it, smelling of money.

Pigeon House Mountain

We climb past mountain ash and wattle,
through the wet forest with its lyrebirds.

The aborigines named the mountain Didthol,
their word for a woman's breast

and these days you can scale the nipple
on vertical ladders, not looking down,

though, if you did, you'd see all the way
from Point Perpendicular to Mount Dromedary.

I prefer the rocks under my feet and the old words,
Ulladulla, Byangee, Croobyar, Budawang.

Jorvik
for Billy

Beneath *Koppari-Gata*
women haggle over fish,
kids play ninepins in the dust,
a man sells combs made out of bones.

Stafkarl, matsveinn, vagga, strond
I tell you that with your blond hair
you have the blood of a Viking
Guthfrith, Ragnald, Sigtrygg, Bloodaxe

An old man squats behind a wicker fence
straining and cursing the onlooker
Meyla krafla mikli thur syr
You laugh and buy a postcard,

your Canberra accent mingling
with Yorkshire, Geordie, Scouse,
with Polish, American, Japanese
while under our feet your ancestors jabber.

They call to you from villages:
Copmanthorpe, Slaithwaite, Langtoft, Threkeld
they shout down from street signs
Goodramgate, Walmgate, Toft Green, Bootham

Sonarson, I'll buy you the Lego Big Ben,
I'll treat you to a Bettys' hot chocolate
but never forget you came from here
Wild Boar Creek, Eoforvik, Jorvik, York.

Learning Curve

See what a trick love is,
how it survives,
not a rose in a kitchen window
but an underground root.

See what a trick death is,
how it gives you back
good as new from the dolls' hospital
in a tissue-lined box.

See what a trick grief is,
how it hides behind a tree
and jumps out in a mask
making you drop all the parcels.

See what a trick time is,
how sometimes it takes a century
to reach midday
as if it were Everest.

'If I'd slept'

If I'd slept well that night
I'd never have crept down

and so wouldn't have found myself
looking at the black lawn,
the white roses,

wouldn't have come face to face
with the moon at the window
pleading to come in,

or have dropped the cup
and watched the moon stoop
to pick up the pieces.

Acute Lymphoblastic Leukaemia

You talk of *the first course* like we're discussing entrées.
What feast is this that can steal your lustrous hair
leaving you thin, yellow, puffy with steroids,
yet cheerful in a bright bandanna?
There's no choice, no à la carte, no specials board.
You've just got to get better. Ten to twenty per cent,
you tell me, don't even make it this far. What's two years
with all that life ahead of you?

You ask me if you've changed;
I shake my head *You're still the same old Ros*
and it's true. Still interested in everyone else, still loving
your garden. And yet there's a difference not to do with
your appearance, your energy, your concentration.
You say you once read that no-one recalls
what happens before the age of four
and all your grandchildren are under three.
Do you think, you ask, *they will remember me?*

When I Heard Your Chemo Hadn't Worked

I had the urge to pick blackcurrants,
why it had to be blackcurrants and not blueberries,
raspberries or strawberries I don't know. We never eat
blackcurrants, I guess because they must be cooked
with added sugar and if you boil the pan dry they stick
like crazy and even if the compote works it stains
and the stains never come out however many times
you put the clothes through the hot wash.
It rained on me so hard I had to park my bike
under a tree and try to shelter though the rain
meant business and hit my back over and over
like my mother that time I flicked water
down the stairs at my brother and didn't know
she'd spent all day painting the landing and hall.
When I got there the notice said Far Field
and I walked miles and there were only blackberries
and I'd set my heart on blackcurrants.
Then I spotted the bushes and there was no-one
else and even though it started to rain again and my shoes
were getting stained purple, I didn't care, just crouched
down and milked the fat black drops into the bowl.

Jug

Your garden in spring was filled with white blossom,
pale crocuses, snowdrops, narcissi
but the day before you died I ordered flowers.

My basket, because I kept pressing *order*
and nothing happened, totalled £311

so I gave up and rang them, ordered a jug,
a simple cottage garden jug of stocks,
salmon pink lisianthus, alchemilla mollis

and three Antique Duett roses. My note said
'with all my love'. The call centre girl asked

What is the occasion? Birthday or a celebration?
I didn't know how to answer.
Do you want kisses and if so how many?

I was mean with my kisses, Ros. I answered *one*.
All that morning I pictured you receiving it.

There was no reply when they knocked.
They left them in the garage.

This Morning at the Arboretum

I hoped to find you there. We do that, don't we?
Go back to places to keen over stones or trees
or, in my case, a little jar of wild flowers,
one of the ones Alastair put on the tables.
You'd have approved. Just daisies and grass.
While no-one was looking I stroked the petals
as if I was touching your face. Just that.
In the background, coffee machine, clatter of cups,
a dog drinking from a bowl as if he was dying of thirst.

Afterwards I walked up the long mown drives
and the grasses either side whispered,
here and there among them a poppy, a geranium,
a purple orchid. It's the month of purple, isn't it?
If you were here you could tell me why. In the wood
a mass of purple foxgloves, growing wild.
I sat on a bench and closed my eyes.
Just a distant plane, a bird's chira chira cheee
bees visiting each mauve flower, the hush of trees.

Seat

for Ros

If you hadn't died I would have rung you
and told you how wet my feet were
standing beside the bench we bought
with its new plaque and those so final dates.

I would have said how lovely
the leaves were, how loud the jets
that screamed overhead, how already
a dog had marked the seat with its paws
while its owner sat and admired the view.

And you'd have said to come round,
that you'd have the kettle on,
that you'd warm some scones.
I can see the butter melting on them,
the steam rising from my cup.

Mum's Foot

You'd walk again
if they'd let you go home.
They say *Maybe.*

Not yet. Now your foot
won't stay put under
the sheet and when I try

to lift it the skin's dry
and cold like it says
on page eight of the leaflet.

I can't meet your eye
for the guilt of not
making it happen.

I talk to your foot,
hold it, stroke it,
say sorry to it.

So thin, so white,
the foot of the girl
in the photo, laughing

and running full
pelt towards the sea.

Jonathan's Flowers

The hospice room attempted cheerfulness
with its blue and lemon striped bedspread,
its cornflower blue walls. But the cancer
took no notice, seeping through her last
clean bra. She wore the stain like a medal.

Beyond the window, beyond the striped lawn,
the orchard of cherry and pear and apple trees,
the newly-planted tub of orange marigolds,
white doves strutting on the old barn roof.

What colour is misery? It will always be
the beige of my mother's dressing gown.
Though she was deaf now to their music,
on the bedside table Jonathan's flowers,
sunflowers, deep red roses sang in the gloom.

The Three Little Words

I nearly didn't say them at all;
as it was I waited till the end,
till you were unconscious.

After I'd said them
I grew bolder, safer,
free to say anything I wanted.

The Holding

You're curled on the floor,
a dying animal

and I rise out of myself
a new ghost walking towards you

and I take you and hold you
as a daughter should.

Waking to confusion
about the geography of the room,

I carry the dream with me,
or a ghost of the dream

down to toast and coffee
till it vanishes with the steam

and there's only the phone
still in its cradle.

To My Sister

Thank you for holding my hand
through all this.

I am very sorry
for stamping on your mouse
when I was three,

for taking your Queenie doll
and bathing her
while you were at Trisha's party,

for wearing your nylons into town
and using your lipstick
while you were out riding.

I never realised you were so nice.

Advent

Oh come, oh come, Emmanuel
There's darkness now at three,
the logs will never crackle on her hearth,
she'll not line up the chestnuts on the grate
or spear a crumpet on a fork to toast.

These are the days my mother couldn't face,
these the trees she'll never drag indoors,
these the holly berries rimed with frost.
this the crisp earth cracking underfoot.

I lift the shoe-box fairy from the dark
and peel a tangerine. The first snow falls.
I jab my thumbnail in. That spurt of juice.
December and the kitchen fills with zest.
These dark days I love the most.

Lightning Source UK Ltd.
Milton Keynes UK
UKOW04f2227120915

258522UK00002B/27/P